Tao Te

道德經

老子

Lao Tzu

Cover: Lao Tzu, legendary writer of the Tao Te Ching, leaves China on a water buffalo. Chinese bronze figure from the 17th century. The Chinese text in the background is the first chapter of the Tao Te ching, the Wang Pi version.

On the previous page is a Chinese woodcut with the same Lao Tzu motif. Above the image are the Chinese signs for Tao Te Ching, literally Way Virtue Classic. Below it are the signs for Lao Tzu, Old Master.

Tao Te Ching

The Classic of the Way and Virtue

道德經

Lao Tzu

Translated by Stefan Stenudd

Stefan Stenudd is a Swedish author, artist, and historian of ideas. He has published a number of books in Swedish as well as English, both fiction and non-fiction. Among the latter are books about Taoism, the cosmology of the Greek philosophers, the Japanese martial arts, life force concepts, and astrology.

In the history of ideas he studies the thought patterns of creation myths, but also Aristotle's Poetics. He is an aikido instructor, 6 dan Aikikai Shihan, Vice Chairman of the International Aikido Federation, member of the Swedish Aikido Grading Committee, and President of the Swedish Budo & Martial Arts Federation. He has his own extensive website:

www.stenudd.com

Also by Stefan Stenudd:
Tao Te Ching: The Taoism of Lao Tzu Explained, 2011.
Cosmos of the Ancients: The Greek Philosophers on Myth and Cosmology, 2007.
Life Energy Encyclopedia, 2009.
Qi: Increase Your Life Energy, 2008.
Aikido Principles, 2008.
Attacks in Aikido, 2008.
Aikibatto: Sword Exercises for Aikido Students, 2007.
Your Health in Your Horoscope, 2009.
All's End, 2007.
Murder, 2006.

Stefan Stenudd's Taoism Website:
www.taoistic.com

Tao Te Ching: The Classic of the Way and Virtue.
Lao Tzu
Copyright © Stefan Stenudd, 2011
Book design by the Stefan Stenudd.
All rights reserved.
ISBN: 978-91-7894-052-3
Publisher: Arriba, Malmö, Sweden, info@arriba.se
www.arriba.se

Contents

Wang Pi	Mawangdui A	Mawangdui B
道可道	道可道也∠	道可道也
非常道	非恆道也∠	口口口
名可名	名可名也‧	口口口
非常名	非恆名也	口恆名也
無名天地之始	無名萬物之始也∠	無名萬物之始也
有名萬物之母	有名萬物之母也口	有名萬物之母也
故常無欲以觀其妙	恆無欲也以觀其眇	故恆無欲也以觀口口口
常有欲以觀其徼	恆有欲也以觀其所	恆又欲也以觀‧所
此兩者同出而異名	嗷兩者同出異名	嗷兩者同出異名
同謂之玄	同胃玄	同胃玄
玄之又玄	之有玄	之又玄
眾妙之門	眾眇之口	眾眇之門

Three versions of the first chapter. Squares mark damaged parts of the text. The chapter is missing in the Guodian manuscript.

Foreword

Lao Tzu is the legendary writer of the Tao Te Ching, The Classic of the Way and Virtue. He is supposed to have lived in the 6th Century BC. Experts disagree on whether he ever existed or not. The Tao Te Ching might be a compilation of separate texts and sayings, without one single author. But then again, it could also be that one man's work.

The name Lao Tzu is honorific. It means Old Master and has also been used traditionally as a title for the Tao Te Ching. It is still in such use among many scholars.

The oldest manuscript of the book found so far is that from Kuo-tien (Guodian), dated to around 300 BC. It is far from complete, but its existence proves that the text appeared no later than in the 4th century BC.

The oldest almost complete versions of the book are the two manuscripts found in Ma-Wang-tui (Mawangdui), from around the year 200 BC, one slightly older than the other. All other manuscripts are significantly younger.

The most widely spread and used version of the Tao Te Ching has for many centuries been the one included in the comments to the text made by Wang Pi, who lived in the 3rd century CE.

The Tao Te Ching is the foremost and oldest text on Taoism. Originally, it had no division into 81 chapters. This was introduced later, probably in the 1st century BC. For most of the book, it is quite obvious and easily defended, but a few chapters have been questioned. A line or two might seem more appropriate in the previous or following chapter, and

Lao Tzu. Ink painting by Mu-ch'i, 13ᵗʰ century.

老子

some chapters might make more sense if split in two. The number of chapters was established to create the symbolic symmetry of 9 X 9.

Already in the Ma-Wang-tui manuscripts, the book had two parts – although in both those manuscripts the order of them was reverse to the presently accepted form. The book's name is derived from these two parts. The first one starts with the word Tao, the Way, and the second part with Te, virtue (actually the expression "highest virtue").

Most of the chapters are rhymed. This was easily accomplished in the Chinese language and with its generous rules for what is considered a rhyme. Translations into other languages rarely try the same, at least not those produced since a couple of decades into the 20th century.

There have been countless translations of the Tao Te Ching. In the Western world, the first one was made by the French priest Francois Noël in the beginning of the 18th century. It was in Latin and passed unnoticed. The first printed version was the French one by Stanislas Julien in 1842. In English, James Legge was the first in 1891. Already by the turn of the century, many other translations into several languages had followed.

Chinese words are transcribed to Western languages in different ways. English Tao Te Ching versions mostly use the Wade-Giles system. Lately, the pinyin system, introduced by the Chinese government in the 1950's, is increasingly used – certainly for modern texts, but also to some extent for the Chinese classics.

Tao Te Ching is the Wade-Giles spelling. In pinyin it would be *Daodejing*. *Lao Tzu* is spelled *Laozi* in pinyin, but there have also been several other ways of spelling his name, for example *Lao Tsu* and *Lao Tse*.

The following translation of the Tao Te Ching is mainly based on these versions: Wang Pi (Wang Bi in pinyin), the two manuscripts of Mawangdui, and that of Guodian. A great number of translations into Western languages, mostly but not only English, have also been consulted.

In the following, the 81 chapters are completely uncommented. I have also published this translation of Lao Tzu's text in a book including comments and explanations: *Tao Te Ching. The Taoism of Lao Tzu Explained* (2011). For other versions of the Tao Te Ching, see the list of literature that ends this book.

Stefan Stenudd
July, 2011

Tao

The Way

1

The Way that can be walked is not the eternal Way.
The name that can be named is not the eternal name.
The nameless is the beginning of Heaven and Earth.
The named is the mother of all things.

Therefore:
Free from desire you see the mystery.
Full of desire you see the manifestations.
These two have the same origin but differ in name.
That is the secret,
The secret of secrets,
The gate to all mysteries.

2

When everyone in the world sees beauty,
Then ugly exists.
When everyone sees good,
Then bad exists.

Therefore:
What is and what is not create each other.
Difficult and easy complement each other.
Tall and short shape each other.
High and low rest on each other.
Voice and tone blend with each other.
First and last follow each other.

So, the sage acts by doing nothing,
Teaches without speaking,
Attends all things without making claim on them,
Works for them without making them dependent,
Demands no honor for his deed.
Because he demands no honor,
He will never be dishonored.

老子

3

Not praising the deserving
Prevents envy.
Not valuing wealth
Prevents theft.
Not displaying what's desirable
Prevents confusion of the senses.

Therefore:
The sage governs by emptying senses and filling bellies,
Curbing strife and strengthening backs,
Keeping the people ignorant and without desire,
Making the learned afraid to act.
If he acts without action, order will prevail.

4

The Way is empty, yet inexhaustible,
Like an abyss!
It seems to be the origin of all things.
It dulls the sharpness,
Unties the knots,
Dims the light,
Becomes one with the dust.

Deeply hidden, as if it only might exist.
I do not know whose child it is.
It seems to precede the ancestor of all.

5

Heaven and Earth are not kind.
They regard all things as offerings.
The sage is not kind.
He regards people as offerings.

Is not the space between Heaven and Earth like a bellows?
It is empty, but lacks nothing.
The more it moves, the more comes out of it.

A multitude of words is tiresome,
Unlike remaining centered.

6

The valley spirit never dies.
It is called the mystical female.
The entrance to the mystical female
Is called the root of Heaven and Earth.

Though gossamer,
As if barely existing,
It is used but never spent.

7

Heaven is eternal and Earth is lasting.
How can they be eternal and lasting?
Because they do not live for themselves.
That is how they can be eternal.

Therefore:
The sage puts himself last and becomes the first,
Neglects himself and is preserved.
Is it not because he is unselfish that he fulfills himself?

8

Supreme good is like water.
Water greatly benefits all things, without conflict.
It flows through places that people loathe.
Thereby it is close to the Way.

A good dwelling is on the ground.
A good mind is deep.
A good gift is kind.
A good word is sincere.
A good ruler is just.
A good worker is able.
A good deed is timely.

Where there is no conflict, there is no fault.

9

Filling all the way to the brim
Is not as good as halting in time.
Pounding an edge to sharpness
Will not make it last.
Keeping plenty of gold and jade in the palace
Makes no one able to defend it.
Displaying riches and titles with pride
Brings about one's downfall.

To retreat after a work well done is Heaven's Way.

10

Can you make your soul embrace the One
And not lose it?
Can you gather your vital breath
And yet be tender like a newborn baby?
Can you clean your inner reflection
And keep it spotless?
Can you care for the people and rule the country
And not be cunning?
Can you open and close the gate of Heaven
And act like a woman?
Can you comprehend everything in the four directions
And still do nothing?

To give birth to them and nourish them,
Carry them without taking possession of them,
Care for them without subduing them,
Raise them without steering them.
That is the greatest virtue.

11

Thirty spokes are joined in the wheel's hub.
The hole in the middle makes it useful.
Mold clay into a bowl.
The empty space makes it useful.
Cut out doors and windows for the house.
The holes make it useful.

Therefore, the value comes from what is there,
But the use comes from what is not there.

12

The five colors blind the eye.
The five tones deafen the ear.
The five flavors dull the mouth.

Racing through the field and hunting make the mind
wild.
Searching for precious goods leads astray.

Therefore, the sage attends to the belly,
And not to what he sees.
He rejects the latter and chooses the former.

老子

13

Praise and disgrace cause fear.
Honor and great distress are like the body.

What does it mean that praise and disgrace cause fear?
Praise leads to weakness.
Getting it causes fear, losing it causes fear.
This is why praise and disgrace cause fear.

What does it mean that honor and great distress are like
the body?
The reason for great distress is the body.
Without it, what distress could there be?

Therefore:
He who treasures his body as much as the world
Can care for the world.
He who loves his body as much as the world
Can be entrusted with the world.

14

Look, it cannot be seen,
So it is called invisible.
Listen, it cannot be heard,
So it is called soundless.
Touch, it cannot be caught,
So it is called elusive.
These three cannot be examined,
So they unite into one.

Above it there is no light,
Below it there is no darkness.
Endlessness beyond description.
It returns to non-existence.
It is called the shapeless shape,
The substance without form.
It is called obscurely evasive.
Meet it and you do not see its beginning,
Follow it and you do not see its end.

Hold on to the ancient Way to master the present,
And to learn the distant beginning.
This is called the unbroken strand of the Way.

老子

15

Ancient masters of excellence had a subtle essence,
And a depth too profound to comprehend.
Because they were impossible to comprehend,
I will try to describe them by their appearance.

Cautious, like crossing a river in the winter.
Wary, as if surrounded by strangers.
Dignified, like a guest.
Yielding, like ice about to melt.
Simple, like uncarved wood.
Open, like a valley.
Obscure, like muddy waters.

Who can wait in stillness while the mud settles?
Who can rest until the moment of action?

He who holds on to the Way seeks no excess.
Since he lacks excess,
He can grow old in no need to be renewed.

16

Attain utmost emptiness.
Abide in steadfast stillness.

All things arise in unison.
Thereby we see their return.
All things flourish,
And each returns to its source.

Returning to the source is stillness.
It is returning to one's fate.
Returning to one's fate is eternal.
Knowledge of the eternal is realization.

Not knowing of the eternal leads to unfortunate errors.
Knowledge of the eternal is all-embracing.
To be all-embracing leads to righteousness,
Which is majestic.
To be majestic leads to the Heavenly.
To be Heavenly leads to the Way.

The Way is eternal.
Until your last day, you are free from peril.

17

The supreme rulers are hardly known by their subjects.
The lesser are loved and praised.
The even lesser are feared.
The least are despised.

Those who show no trust will not be trusted.
Those who are quiet value the words.
When their task is completed, people will say:
We did it ourselves.

18

When the great Tao is abandoned,
Benevolence and righteousness arise.
When wisdom and knowledge appear,
Great pretense arises.
When family ties are disturbed,
Devoted children arise.
When people are unsettled,
Loyal ministers arise.

老子

19

Abandon wisdom, discard knowledge,
And people will benefit a hundredfold.
Abandon benevolence, discard duty,
And people will return to the family ties.
Abandon cleverness, discard profit,
And thieves and robbers will disappear.

These three, though, are superficial, and not enough.
Let this be what to rely on:

Behave simply and hold on to purity.
Lessen selfishness and restrain desires.
Abandon knowledge and your worries are over.

20

What's the difference between yes and no?
What's the difference between beautiful and ugly?
Must one dread what others dread?
Oh barbarity! Will it never end?

Other people are joyous, like on the feast of the ox,
Like on the way up to the terrace in the spring.
I alone am inert, giving no sign,
Like a newborn baby who has not learned to smile.
I am wearied, as if I lacked a home to go to.

Other people have more than they need,
I alone seem wanting.
I have the mind of a fool,
Understanding nothing.

The common people see clearly,
I alone am held in the dark.
The common people are sharp,
Only I am clumsy,
Like drifting on the waves of the sea,
Without direction.

Other people are occupied,
I alone am unwilling, like the outcast.
I alone am different from the others,
Because I am nourished by the great mother.

老子

21

The greatest virtue is to follow the Way utterly.
Its nature is utterly vague and evasive.
How evasive and vague!
Yet its center has form.
How vague and evasive!
Yet its center has substance.
How deep and obscure!
Yet its center has essence.
This essence is real,
So, its center can be trusted.

From now back to antiquity,
Its name has not been lost.
Thereby, see the origin of all.
How do I know it is the origin of all?
By this.

22

Hulk to be whole.
Bend to be straight.
Empty to be filled.
Wear down to be renewed.
Reduce to gain.
Excess confuses.

Therefore, the sage embraces the one,
And is an example to the world.
He does not show off, therefore he shines.
He does not justify himself, therefore he is revered.
He does not boast, therefore he is honored.
He does not praise himself, therefore he remains.
Because he opposes no one,
No one in the world can oppose him.

The ancients said:
Hulk to be whole.
Are these just empty words?
Indeed, he shall remain whole.

23

To be of few words is natural.

Strong winds do not last all morning,
Hard rains do not last all day.
What cause them?
Heaven and Earth.
If Heaven and Earth are unable to persist,
How could man?

Those who follow the Way are one with the Way.
Those who live virtuously are one with virtue.
Those who deprive themselves are one with deprivation.

Those who are one with the Way are welcomed by the
Way.
Those who are one with virtue are welcomed by virtue.
Those who are one with deprivation are deprived of
deprivation.

Those who do not show trust will not be trusted.

24

Those who stand on their toes are not steady.
Those who take long steps cannot keep the pace.
Those who show off do not shine.
Those who are self-righteous are not prominent.
Those who boast are not respected.
Those who praise themselves do not prevail.

To the Way,
Such people are surplus provisions and useless actions.
They are rejected by many.
Therefore:
Those who follow the Way do not remain with them.

25

There was something that finished chaos,
Born before Heaven and Earth.
So silent and still!
So pure and deep!
It stands alone and immutable,
Ever-present and inexhaustible.
It can be called the mother of the whole world.
I do not know its name. I call it the Way.
For the lack of better words I call it great.

Great means constant flow.
Constant flow means far-reaching.
Far-reaching means returning.

That is how the Way is great.
Heaven is great,
Earth is great,
And the king is also great.
In the world there are four greats,
And the king is one of them.

Man is ruled by Earth.
Earth is ruled by Heaven.
Heaven is ruled by the Way.
The Way is ruled by itself.

26

Heavy is the root of light.
Stillness is the ruler of haste.

Therefore:
Although he travels all day,
The sage never loses sight of his luggage carts.
Only when he rests securely inside the walls,
He relaxes his attention.

Why would a ruler with ten thousand chariots
Look lightly on himself or his domain?
In lightness the root is lost.
In haste the ruler is lost.

27

A good wanderer leaves no trace.
A good speaker does not stutter.
A good counter needs no calculator.
A good door needs no lock,
Still it can't be opened.
A good mooring needs no knot,
Still no one can untie it.

Therefore the sage takes care of all people,
Forsaking no one.
He takes care of all things,
Forsaking nothing.
This is called following the light.

So, a good person is the bad person's teacher.
A bad person is the good person's task.
The one who does not honor the teacher
And the one who does not honor the task,
Although ever so knowledgeable,
They are confused.
This is called the subtle essence.

28

Knowing the manly, but clinging to the womanly,
You become the valley of the world.
Being the valley of the world,
Eternal virtue will never desert you,
And you become like a little child anew.

Knowing the bright, but clinging to the dark,
You become a model to the world.
Being a model to the world,
Eternal virtue will never falter in you,
And you return to the boundless.

Knowing honor, but clinging to disgrace,
You become the valley of the world.
Being the valley of the world,
Eternal virtue will be full in you,
And you return to the state of uncarved wood.

When the uncarved wood is split,
Its parts are put to use.
When the sage is put to use,
He becomes the head.
The best way to carve is not to split.

29

Conquering the world and changing it,
I do not think it can succeed.
The world is a sacred vessel that cannot be changed.
He who changes it will destroy it.
He who seizes it will lose it.

So, among all things,
Some lead and some follow,
Some sigh and some pant,
Some are strong and some are weak,
Some overcome and some succumb.

Therefore the sage avoids extremity, excess, and
extravagance.

30

Those who advice the ruler on the Way,
Do not want the world subdued with weapons.
Such deeds bring on retaliation.
Thorn bushes grow where armies have camped.
Battles are followed by years of famine.
Therefore, good leaders reach solutions,
And then stop.
They do not dare to rely on force.

Solutions without arrogance,
Solutions without scorn,
Solutions without pride,
Solutions without benefit,
Solutions without domination.

Things exalted then decay.
This is going against the Way.
What goes against the Way meets an early end.

31

Weapons are ominous tools.
They are abhorred by all creatures.
Anyone who follows the Way shuns them.

In peaceful times, the noble ruler honors the left side.
At war, he honors the right side.

Weapons are ominous tools.
They are not the noble ruler's tools.
He only uses them when he can't avoid it.
Peace and quiet are preferred.
Victory should not be praised.
Those who praise victory relish manslaughter.
Those who relish manslaughter
Cannot reach their goals in the world.

At times of joy, the left side is honored.
At times of grief, the right side is honored.
At battle, the second in command stands to the left,
And the commander in chief to the right.
This means they stand as in funerals.

When many people are killed
They should be mourned and lamented.
Those who are victorious in war
Should follow the rites of funerals.

32

The Way is ever nameless.
Though simple and subtle,
The world cannot lead it.
If princes and kings could follow it,
All things would by themselves abide,
Heaven and Earth would unite
And sweet dew would fall.
People would by themselves find harmony,
Without being commanded.

As soon as rules were made, names were given.
There are already many names.
One must know when it is enough.
Those who know when it is enough will not perish.

What the Way is to the world,
The stream is to the river and the sea.

33

Those who understand others are clever,
Those who understand themselves are wise.
Those who defeat others are strong,
Those who defeat themselves are mighty.

Those who know when they have enough are rich.
Those who are unswerving have resolve.
Those who stay where they are will endure.
Those who die without being forgotten get longevity.

34

The great Way is all-pervading.
It reaches to the left and to the right.
All things depend on it with their existence.
Still it demands no obedience.
It demands no honor for what it accomplishes.
It clothes and feeds all things without ruling them.

It is eternally without desire.
So, it can be called small.
All things return to it,
Although it does not make itself their ruler.
So, it can be called great.

Therefore, the sage does not strive to be great.
Thereby he can accomplish the great.

老子

35

Hold on to the great image,
And the whole world follows,
Follows unharmed,
Content and completely at peace.

Music and food make the traveler halt.
But words spoken about the Way have no taste.
When looked at, there's not enough to see.
When listened to, there's not enough to hear.
When used, it is never exhausted.

36

What should be shrunken must first be stretched.
What should be weakened must first be strengthened.
What should be abolished must first be cherished.
What should be deprived must first be enriched.

This is called understanding the hidden.
The soft and weak overcome the hard and strong.

The fish cannot leave the deep waters.
The state's weaponry should not be displayed.

老子

37

The Way is ever without action,
Yet nothing is left undone.
If princes and kings can abide by this,
All things will form themselves.
If they form themselves and desires arise,
I subdue them with nameless simplicity.
Nameless simplicity will indeed free them from desires.

Without desire there is stillness,
And the world settles by itself.

Te

Virtue

38

The highest virtue is not virtuous.
Therefore it has virtue.
The lowest virtue holds on to virtue.
Therefore it has no virtue.

The highest virtue does nothing.
Yet, nothing needs to be done.
The lowest virtue does everything.
Yet, much remains to be done.

The highest benevolence acts without purpose.
The highest righteousness acts with purpose.
The highest ritual acts, but since no one cares,
It raises its arms and uses force.

Therefore, when the Way is lost there is virtue.
When virtue is lost there is benevolence.
When benevolence is lost there is righteousness.
When righteousness is lost there are rituals.
Rituals are the end of fidelity and honesty,
And the beginning of confusion.

Knowing the future is the flower of the Way,
And the beginning of folly.
Therefore,
The truly great ones rely on substance,
And not on surface,
Hold on to the fruit,
And not to the flower.
They reject the latter and receive the former.

39

These things of old obtained unity with the one.
Heaven obtained unity and became clear.
Earth obtained unity and became firm.
The spirits obtained unity and became deities.
The valleys obtained unity and became abundant.
All things obtained unity and became animate.
Princes and kings obtained unity and became rulers of the world.
They all obtained unity with the one.

If Heaven were not clear it might rend.
If Earth were not firm it might crumble.
If the spirits were not deities they might wither.
If the valleys were not abundant they might dry up.
If all things were not animate they might perish.
If princes and kings were not exalted they might be overthrown.

Therefore:
The noble must make humility his root.
The high must make the low its base.
That is why princes and kings call themselves orphaned, desolate, unworthy.
Is that not to make humility their root?

The separate parts make no carriage.
So, do not strive for the shine of jade,
But clatter like stone.

40

Returning is the movement of the Way.
Yielding is the manner of the Way.

All things in the world are born out of being.
Being is born out of non-being.

41

The superior student listens to the Way
And follows it closely.
The average student listens to the Way
And follows some and some not.
The lesser student listens to the Way
And laughs out loud.
If there were no laughter it would not be the Way.

So, it has been said:
The light of the Way seems dim.
The progress of the Way seems retreating.
The straightness of the Way seems curved.
The highest virtue seems as low as a valley.
The purest white seems stained.
The grandest virtue seems deficient.
The sturdiest virtue seems fragile.
The most fundamental seems fickle.
The perfect square lacks corners.
The greatest vessel takes long to complete.
The highest tone is hard to hear.
The great image lacks shape.

The Way is hidden and nameless.
Still only the Way nourishes and completes.

老子

42

The Way gave birth to one.
One gave birth to two.
Two gave birth to three.
Three gave birth to all things.

All things carry yin and embrace yang.
They reach harmony by blending with the vital breath.

What people loathe the most
Is to be orphaned, desolate, unworthy.
But this is what princes and kings call themselves.
Sometimes gain comes from losing,
And sometimes loss comes from gaining.

What others have taught, I also teach:
The forceful and violent will not die from natural causes.
This will be my chief doctrine.

43

The softest in the world
Surpasses the hardest in the world.
What has no substance
Can penetrate what has no opening.

Thereby I know the value of non-action.

The value of teaching without words
And accomplishing without action
Is understood by few in the world.

44

Your name or your body,
What is dearer?
Your body or your wealth,
What is worthier?
Gain or loss,
What is worse?

Greed is costly.
Assembled fortunes are lost.
Those who are content suffer no disgrace.
Those who know when to halt are unharmed.
They last long.

45

The most complete seems lacking.
Yet in use it is not exhausted.
The most abundant seems empty.
Yet in use it is not drained.

The most straight seems curved.
The most able seems clumsy.
The most eloquent seems to stutter.

Movement overcomes cold.
Stillness overcomes heat.
Peace and quiet govern the world.

老子

46

When the Way governs the world,
The proud stallions drag dung carriages.
When the Way is lost to the world,
War horses are bred outside the city.

There is no greater crime than desire.
There is no greater disaster than discontent.
There is no greater misfortune than greed.

Therefore:
To have enough of enough is always enough.

47

Without stepping out the door,
You can know the world.
Without looking through the window,
You can see Heaven's Way.
The longer you travel, the less you know.

Therefore:
The sage knows without traveling,
Perceives without looking,
Completes without acting.

老子

48

Those who seek knowledge,
Collect something every day.
Those who seek the Way,
Let go of something every day.

They let go and let go,
Until reaching no action.
When nothing is done,
Nothing is left undone.

Never take over the world to tamper with it.
Those who want to tamper with it
Are not fit to take over the world.

49

The sage has no concern for himself,
But makes the concerns of others his own.

He is good to those who are good.
He is also good to those who are not good.
That is the virtue of good.
He is faithful to people who are faithful.
He is also faithful to people who are not faithful.
That is the virtue of faithfulness.

The sage is one with the world,
And lives in harmony with it.
People turn their eyes and ears to him,
And the sage cares for them like his own children.

50

We go from birth to death.
Three out of ten follow life.
Three out of ten follow death.
People who rush from birth to death
Are also three out of ten.
Why is that so?
Because they want to make too much of life.

I have heard that the one who knows how to live
Can wander through the land
Without encountering the rhinoceros or the tiger.
He passes the battlefield
Without being struck by weapons.
In him, the rhinoceros finds no opening for its horn.
The tiger finds no opening for its claws.
The soldiers find no opening for their blades.

Why is that so?
Death has no place in him.

51

The Way gives birth to them.
Virtue gives them nourishment.
Matter gives them shape.
Conditions make them whole.

Therefore:
Of all things,
None does not revere the Way and honor virtue.
Reverence of the Way and honoring virtue
Were not demanded of them,
But it is in their nature.

So, the Way gives birth to them,
Nourishes them,
Raises them,
Nurtures them,
Protects them,
Matures them,
Takes care of them.
It gives birth without seizing,
Helps without claim,
Fosters without ruling.
This is called the profound virtue.

52

The world's beginning is its mother.
To have found the mother
Is also to know the children.
Although you know the children,
Cling to the mother.
Until your last day you will not be harmed.

Seal the openings, shut the doors,
And until your last day you will not be exhausted.
Widen the openings, interfere,
And until your last day you will not be safe.

Seeing the small is called clarity.
Holding on to the weak is called strength.
Use the light to return to clarity.
Then you will not cause yourself misery.
This is called following the eternal.

53

If I have just an ounce of sense,
I follow the great Way,
And fear only to stray from it.
The great Way is very straight,
But people prefer to deviate.

When the palace is magnificent,
The fields are filled with weeds,
And the granaries are empty.
Some have lavish garments,
Carry sharp swords,
And feast on food and drink.
They possess more than they can spend.
This is called the vanity of robbers.

It is certainly not the Way.

54

What is well planted will not be uprooted.
What is well held will not escape.
Children and grandchildren will not cease to praise it.

Cultivate virtue in yourself,
And it will be true.
Cultivate virtue in the family,
And it will be overflowing.
Cultivate virtue in the town,
And it will be lasting.
Cultivate virtue in the country,
And it will be abundant.
Cultivate virtue in the world,
And it will be universal.

Therefore:
See others as yourself.
See families as your family.
See towns as your town.
See countries as your country.
See worlds as your world.

How do I know that the world is such?
By this.

55

The one who is filled by virtue is like a newborn baby.
Wasps, scorpions, and serpents will not sting him.
Birds of prey and wild beasts will not strike him.
His bones are soft, his muscles weak,
But his grasp is firm.
He has not experienced the union of man and woman,
Still his penis rises.
His manhood is at its very height.
He can shout all day without getting hoarse.
His harmony is at its very height.

Harmony is called the eternal.
Knowing the eternal is called clarity.
Filling life exceedingly is called ominous.
Letting the mind control the vital breath is called force.

Things exalted then decay.
This is going against the Way.
What goes against the Way meets an early end.

56

Those who know it do not speak about it.
Those who speak about it do not know it.

Seal the openings.
Shut the doors.
Dull the sharpness.
Untie the knots.
Dim the light.
Become one with the dust.
This is called the profound union.

Those who obtain it
Can neither be seduced nor abandoned.
Those who obtain it
Can neither be favored nor neglected.
Those who obtain it
Can neither be honored nor humiliated.
Therefore, they are the most esteemed in the world.

57

Use justice to rule a country.
Use surprise to wage war.
Use non-action to govern the world.

How do I know it is so?
As for the world,
The more restrictions and prohibitions there are,
The poorer the people will be.
The more sharp weapons people have in a country,
The bigger the disorder will be.
The more clever and cunning people are,
The stranger the events will be.
The more laws and commands there are,
The more thieves and robbers there will be.

Therefore the sage says:
I do not act,
And people become reformed by themselves.
I am at peace,
And people become fair by themselves.
I do not interfere,
And people become rich by themselves.
I have no desire to desire,
And people become like the uncarved wood by
themselves.

老子

58

When the government is quite unobtrusive,
People are indeed pure.
When the government is quite prying,
People are indeed conniving.

Misery is what happiness rests upon.
Happiness is what misery lurks beneath.
Who knows where it ends?
Is there nothing correct?
Correct becomes defect.
Good becomes ominous.
People's delusions have certainly lasted long.

Therefore the sage is sharp but does not cut,
Pointed but does not pierce,
Forthright but does not offend,
Bright but does not dazzle.

59

When leading people and serving Heaven,
Nothing exceeds moderation.
Truly, moderation means prevention.
Prevention means achieving much virtue.

When much virtue is achieved,
Nothing is not overcome.
Nothing not overcome means
Nobody knows the limits.
When nobody knows the limits,
One can rule the country.

The one who rules like the mother lasts long.
This is called deep roots and a solid base,
the Way to long life and clarity.

老子

60

Ruling a great country is like cooking a small fish.

When the world is ruled according to the Way,
The ghosts lose their power.
The ghosts do not really lose their power,
But it is not used to harm people.

Not only will their power not harm people,
Nor will the sage harm people.
Since neither of them causes harm,
Unified virtue is restored.

61

A great country is like the lower outlet of a river.
It is the world's meeting ground, the world's female.

The female always surpasses the male with stillness.
In her stillness she is yielding.

Therefore:
If a great country yields to a small country,
It will conquer the small country.
If a small country yields to a great country,
It will be conquered by the great country.
So, some who yield become conquerors,
And some who yield get conquered.

A great country needs more people to serve it.
A small country needs more people to serve.
So, if both shall get what they need,
The great country ought to yield.

老子

62

The Way is the source of all things,
Good people's treasure and bad people's refuge.

Fine words are traded.
Noble deeds gain respect.
But people who are not good,
Why abandon them?

So, when the emperor is crowned
Or the three dukes are appointed,
Rather than sending a gift of jade
Carried by four horses,
Remain still and offer the Way.

Why did the ancients praise the Way?
Did they not say it was because you find what you seek
And are saved from your wrongdoings?
That is why the world praises it.

63

Act without action.
Pursue without interfering.
Taste the tasteless.

Make the small big and the few many.
Return animosity with virtue.
Meet the difficult while it is easy.
Meet the big while it is small.

The most difficult in the world
Must be easy in its beginning.
The biggest in the world
Is small in its beginning.
So, the sage never strives for greatness,
And can therefore accomplish greatness.

Lightly given promises
Must meet with little trust.
Taking things lightly
Must lead to big difficulties.
So, the sage regards things as difficult,
And thereby avoids difficulty.

老子

64

Stillness is easy to maintain.
What has not yet emerged is easy to prevent.
The brittle is easy to shatter.
The small is easy to scatter.
Solve it before it happens.
Order it before chaos emerges.

A tree as wide as a man's embrace
Grows from a tiny shoot.
A tower of nine stories
Starts with a pile of dirt.
A climb of eight hundred feet
Starts where the foot stands.

Those who act will fail.
Those who seize will lose.
So, the sage does not act and therefore does not fail,
Does not seize and therefore does not lose.
People fail at the threshold of success.
Be as cautious at the end as at the beginning.
Then there will be no failure.

Therefore the sage desires no desire,
Does not value rare treasures,
Learns without learning,
Recovers what people have left behind.
He wants all things to follow their own nature,
But dares not act.

65

In ancient times,
Those who followed the Way
Did not try to give people knowledge thereof,
But kept them ignorant.
People are difficult to rule
Because of their knowledge.

To rule by knowledge ravages the country.
To rule not by knowledge blesses the country.
To understand these two is to have precept.
To always have precept is called profound virtue.

Profound virtue is indeed deep and wide.
It leads all things back to the great order.

老子

66

The river and the sea can be kings of a hundred valleys,
Because they lie below them.
That is why they can be the kings of a hundred valleys.

Therefore:
If the sage wants to stand above people,
He must speak to them from below.
If he wants to lead people,
He must follow them from behind.

Therefore:
When the sage stands above people,
They are not oppressed.
When he leads people,
They are not obstructed.
The world will exalt him
And not grow tired of him.

Because he does not resist,
None in the world resists him.

67

The whole world says that my Way is great like nothing
else.
It is great because it is like nothing else.
If it were like everything else,
It would long ago have become insignificant.

I have three treasures that I cherish.
The first is compassion.
The second is moderation.
The third is not claiming to be first in the world.

By compassion one can be brave.
By moderation one can be generous.
By not claiming to be first in the world one can rule.

But to be brave without compassion,
Generous without moderation,
And rule without refraining from being first in the world
Are certain deaths.

So, those who have compassion when they do battle
Will be victorious.
Those who likewise defend themselves
Will be safe.
Heaven will rescue and protect them with compassion.

68

Excellent warriors are not violent.
Excellent soldiers are not furious.
Excellent conquerors do not engage.
Excellent leaders of people lower themselves.

This is called the virtue of no strife.
This is called the use of people's capacity.
This is called the union with Heaven.
It is the perfection of the ancients.

69

Warriors say:
I dare not be like the host,
But would rather be like the guest.
I dare not advance an inch,
But would rather retreat a foot.

This is called marching without marching,
Grabbing without arms,
Charging without enemy,
Seizing without weapons.

No misfortune is worse
Than underestimating the enemy.
Underestimating the enemy,
I risk losing my treasure.
Therefore:
When equal armies battle,
The grieving one will be victorious.

老子

70

My words are very easy to understand
And very easy to practice.
Still, no one in the world
Can understand or practice them.

My words have an origin.
My deeds have a sovereign.
Truly, because people do not understand this,
They do not understand me.

That so few understand me is why I am treasured.
Therefore, the sage wears coarse clothes, concealing jade.

71

Knowing that you do not know is the best.
Not knowing that you do not know is an illness.

Truly, only those who see illness as illness
Can avoid illness.
The sage is not ill,
Because he sees illness as illness.
Therefore he is not ill.

72

When people do not dread authorities,
Then a greater dread descends.

Do not crowd their dwellings.
Do not make them weary at their work.
If you do not make them weary,
They will not be weary of you.

Therefore, the sage knows himself,
But does not parade.
He cherishes himself,
But does not praise himself.
He discards the one,
And chooses the other.

73

Those who have the courage to dare will perish.
Those who have the courage not to dare will live.
Of those two, one is beneficial and one is harmful.
What Heaven detests, who knows why?
Even the sage considers it difficult.

Heaven's Way does not contend,
Yet it certainly triumphs.
It does not speak,
Yet it certainly answers.
It does not summon,
Yet things come by themselves.
It seems to be at rest,
Yet it certainly has a plan.

Heaven's net is very vast.
It is sparsely meshed, yet nothing slips through.

老子

74

If people are not afraid of dying,
Why threaten them with death?
If people live in constant fear of death,
And if breaking the law is punished by death,
Then who would dare?

There is one appointed supreme executioner.
Truly, trying to take the place of the supreme executioner
Is like trying to carve wood like a master carpenter.
Of those who try to carve wood like a master carpenter,
There are few who do not injure their hands.

75

People starve.
The rulers consume too much with their taxes.
That is why people starve.

People are hard to govern.
The rulers interfere with too much.
That is why people are hard to govern.

People take death lightly.
They expect too much of life.
That is why people take death lightly.

Truly, only acting without thought of one's life
Is superior to valuing one's life.

老子

76

People are born soft and weak.
They die hard and stiff.
All things such as grass and trees
Are soft and supple in life.
At their death they are withered and dry.

So, the hard and stiff are death's companions.
The soft and weak are life's companions.

Therefore:
The unyielding army will not win.
The rigid tree will be felled.
The rigid and big belong below.
The soft and weak belong above.

77

Heaven's Way is like stretching a bow.
The high is lowered and the low is raised.
Excess is reduced and deficiency is replenished.

Heaven's Way reduces excess and replenishes deficiency.
People's Way is not so.
They reduce the deficient and supply the excessive.
Who has excess and supplies the world?
Only the one who follows the Way.

Therefore, the sage acts without taking credit.
He accomplishes without dwelling on it.
He does not want to display his worth.

78

Nothing in the world is softer and weaker than water.
Yet, to attack the hard and strong,
Nothing surpasses it.
Nothing can take its place.

The weak overcomes the strong.
The soft overcomes the hard.
Everybody in the world knows this,
Still nobody makes use of it.

Therefore the sage says:
To bear the country's disgrace
Is to rule the shrines of soil and grain.
To bear the country's misfortunes
Is to be the king of the world.

True words seem false.

79

When bitter enemies make peace,
Surely some bitterness remains.
How can this be solved?

Therefore:
The sage honors his part of the settlement,
But does not exact his due from others.
The virtuous carry out the settlement,
But those without virtue pursue their claims.

Heaven's Way gives no favors.
It always remains with good people.

80

Let the country be small,
And the inhabitants few.

Although there are weapons
For tens and hundreds of soldiers,
They will not be used.
Let people take death seriously,
And not travel far.
Although they have boats and carriages,
There's no occasion to use them.
Although they have armor and weapons,
There's no occasion to wear them.
Let people return to making knots on ropes,
Instead of writing.

Their food will be tasty.
Their clothes will be comfortable.
Their homes will be tranquil.
They will rejoice in their daily life.

They can see their neighbors.
Roosters and dogs can be heard from there.
Still, they will age and die
Without visiting one another.

81

True words are not pleasing.
Pleasing words are not true.
Those who are right do not argue.
Those who argue are not right.
Those who know are not learned.
Those who are learned do not know.

The sage does not hoard.
The more he does for others,
The more he has.
The more he thereby gives to others,
The ever more he gets.

Heaven's Way
Is to benefit and not to harm.
The sage's Way
Is to act and not to contend.

Ching, classic. Calligraphy by the translator.

Literature

There's a forest of books about Taoism, Lao Tzu, and the *Tao Te Ching*. It makes no sense to list them all, so I have chosen a few versions of the *Tao Te Ching* that I value or find significant in the continued exploration of Lao Tzu's thoughts. Less important works are also included, if they appeared before the present flood of Taoism texts emerged.

The subject is a hot one, so new books will appear as you read this, but I believe that some of the sources listed below will not that quickly be obsolete.

I have added a short comment to every version listed. It's just my personal opinion, so don't trust it any longer than you find it useful. Once you have started your own exploration of the subject, there's no guide more trustworthy than your own inkling.

As for the resources on the Internet, they change so quickly that I can only recommend a Google search (or whatever search engine is the most prominent one, when you read this). Notice that different spellings give partly different search results. For example, *Tao Te Ching*, *Dao De Jing*, and *Daodejing* searches differ, although the major search engines regard them as synonymous. The same is true for *Lao Tzu*, *Lao Zi*, and *Laozi*. Many complete translations of the *Tao Te Ching* are available on the Internet.

Tao Te Ching Versions

Ames, Roger T. & Hall, David L.: DAO DE JING
New York, Ballantine 2003.
A knowledgeable and rather daring version, which also presents the text in Chinese. The findings in Guodian are richly presented and included in the interpretation.

Blakney, Raymond B.: LAO TZU
USA, New American Library 1955.
A straightforward and clear version of the text, with elaborate comments and explanations.

Bynner, Witter: THE WAY OF LIFE ACCORDING TO
LAOTZU
New York, Day 1944.
An American version, which is also its subtitle. It's based on English versions of that time. In the effort to clarify the chapters, he allows himself to deviate quite far from Lao Tzu's text.

Chen, Ellen M.: THE TAO TE CHING
New York, Paragon 1989.
With a knowledge that is only surpassed by the categorical attitude, Chen presents a version that includes but is far from dominated by the Mawangdui manuscripts. Lots of facts are also included, as well as far-reaching personal interpretations of Taoist philosophy and how to apply it.

Cheng, Man-jan: LAO TZU: MY WORDS ARE VERY EASY
TO UNDERSTAND
California, North Atlantic Books 1981. Translated to English by
Tam C. Gibbs.
Cheng comments the chapters of the text in short lessons, focused on the principles of Taoism. The explanations are so short that they don't add much to the text itself. The Chinese text is included in the book.

Cleary, Thomas: THE ESSENTIAL TAO
San Francisco, Harper Collins 1993.

The East Asian Studies PhD has translated several Taoist and Buddhist texts, which have been published in a number of different volumes. This one contains the texts of both Lao Tzu and Chuang Tzu. His translation is competent, although his choice of words is sometimes odd, deviating from the usual solutions.

Crowley, Aleister: THE TAO TEH KING
1918. Several editions in print.
The famous occultist made his own very personal interpretation of the text, where the hexagrams of *I Ching* have also been used. Crowley is always worth reading, although it's not certain that he speaks according to the Tao of Lao Tzu.

Duyvendak, J.J.L.: TAO TE CHING
London, Murray 1954.
This professor in Chinese fills his version of the text with elaborate comments, including linguistic and philosophical aspects. This version is one of the few that met the approval of the prominent sinologist Bernhard Karlgren.

Feng, Gia-fu & English, Jane: LAO TSU: TAO TE CHING
London, Wildwood 1973.
This version is simple and rewarding, although it isn't always in accordance with prevalent opinion. It lacks commentaries, but is richly illustrated with both calligraphy of the chapters and mood-filled photographs.

Henricks, Robert: TE-TAO CHING
New York, Ballantine 1989.
The professor of religion manages a very trustworthy version of the text, based primarily on the manuscripts of Ma-

wangdui. Because of their order, he has reversed the words of the title. His comments are knowledgeable and precise. The Mawangdui texts in Chinese are also included. This is a major work on the Mawangdui findings.

Henricks, Robert: LAO TZU'S TAO TE CHING
New York, Columbia University Press 2000.
In this book, Henricks concentrates on the findings in Guodian, which are competently presented and examined. They are also compared to the Mawangdui and Wang Pi versions. The texts are included in Chinese. The problem with the book is that the order of the chapters is according to the findings, which makes it difficult to use as a reference. Hopefully, Henricks finds a solution for it in a coming edition.

Ivanhoe, Philip J.: THE DAODEJING OF LAOZI
Indianapolis, Hackett 2002.
The historian of Chinese thought has made a straightforward and clean translation of the text, a learned introduction to it, and comparisons between other translations. There are also many informative notes.

Jiyu, Ren: A TAOIST CLASSIC: THE BOOK OF LAO ZI
Beijing, Foreign Languages Press 1993.
This Chinese version translated to English also contains precise explanations that focus on how to understand the philosophy of the text and of Taoism. The interpretation and the perspectives are frequently quite far from those of most Western translators, which makes the book particularly interesting to study.

Julien, Stanislas: LE LIVRE DE LA VOIE ET DE LA VERTU Paris 1842.

Julien was a professor in Chinese at the Paris University. His French version is the first printed one in a Western language. It is still in print, as a facsimile. Unfortunately, no English translation of it seems to be in print.

Karlgren, Bernhard: NOTES ON LAO-TSE Bulletin of Östasiatiska Museet, nr. 47/1975. Offprint.

The world famous Swedish sinologist finally published, just three years before his demise, a version of the text. He did so in a way as modest as was his habit – in a magazine of the Stockholm East Asian Museum. His interpretation is precise and clarifying, but the comments are minimal. At the time of his interpretation, the findings in Mawangdui were not at his disposal.

Lau, D.C.: LAO TZU: TAO TE CHING London, Penguin 1963.

This professor of Chinese literature gives a knowledgeable and clear interpretation of the text. The book also contains explicit comments and explanations. In later editions of this book, Lau includes the findings in Mawangdui and Guodian.

Legge, James: THE TAO TEH KING London, Oxford 1891.

Legge's historically significant version has extensive explanations with many references to the Chinese pictograms and their meaning. Still, his translation is aged, especially because of its effort to create poetry, which makes it deviate considerably from the wording of the original.

Le Guin, Ursula K., and Seaton, J. P.: LAO TZU: TAO TE CHING
Boston, Shambhala 1997.
The famous fantasy and science fiction writer has made an elegant and very clear version of the text, in collaboration with a professor of Chinese. There are some comments, especially on how the chapters should be understood and on some linguistic aspects.

Mair, Victor H.: TAO TE CHING
New York, Bantam 1990.
This professor of Chinese bases his interpretation on the Mawangdui manuscripts. The books also contains extensive comments, especially those comparing the text with the ideas of ancient India.

Maurer, Herrymon: TAO: THE WAY OF THE WAYS
England, Wildwood 1986.
These interpretations and comments are aimed at explaining the text's spiritual content, which is done quite cryptically at times. In spite of the late date of this version, Maurer is unfamiliar with the Mawangdui manuscripts.

Mitchell, Stephen: TAO TE CHING: A NEW ENGLISH VERSION
USA, Harper & Row 1988.
This version, with very limited comments, seems to be made without noticeable knowledge of the Mawangdui manuscripts. Still, it has its merits as a simple and direct interpretation of the text. Later editions have made it to the bestseller lists.

Ryden, Edmund: LAOZI: DAODEJING
Oxford University Press 2008.
This version includes the Mawangdui and Guodian findings. The introduction and comments are learned, but the
wording in the translation sometimes gives the impression
of being dated. Ryden translates *Te* as "the life force," which
is similar to Arthur Waley's choice of "the power."

Star, Jonathan: TAO TE CHING
New York, Tarcher Penguin 2001.
The subtitle says that this is the definitive edition, which can
be discussed. But its material is very rich. The interpretation
of the text is given in Star's own words, but also word by
word parallel to the Chinese signs – completely according
to the Wang Pi version. There is also some other valuable
material in the book. It is quite useful to the devoted student
of the *Tao Te Ching*. In spite of its late publishing date, the
Guodian manuscript seems unknown to the author. That
might be corrected in later editions.

Ta-Kao, Chu: TAO TE CHING
London, Mandala 1959.
Ta-Kao allows himself to rearrange the text according to
what he feels is the most probable. That can be discussed.
Otherwise, his interpretation is straightforward and clear.
The comments are sparse.

Wagner, Rudolf G.: A CHINESE READING OF THE
DAODEJING
Albany, State University of New York Press 2003.
This is a translation of the Wang Pi commented version of
the *Tao Te Ching*, which is the most cherished one in Chinese

literature, a classic in its own right. The translation is very competently done, and so are the expert comments. The Chinese text is included. A must for the study of Wang Pi as well as Lao Tzu, but not an easy book to digest.

Waley, Arthur: THE WAY AND ITS POWER
London, Unwin 1934.
Waley's cherished version is assisted by elaborate comments and a long introduction. His interpretations of the chapters are not always the most probable, but his book has won the respect of several important sinologists.

Wilhelm, Richard: TAO TE CHING
London, Arkana 1985. Translated by H.G. Ostwald.
The first edition of Wilhelm's important interpretation in German was published in 1910. In later editions it was re-worked considerably. The comments from 1925 are elaborate about both the language aspects and the ideas of the text. Wilhelm also made a widely spread version of the *I Ching*, where he had C. G. Jung write the foreword. It's a pity he didn't do the same with the *Tao Te Ching*.

Wing, R. L.: THE TAO OF POWER
New York, Doubleday 1986.
This version includes the Chinese writing, also calligraphy as well as other illustrations of interest. The writer has allowed himself the freedom of adapting some of the wordings to modern concepts. The findings in Mawangdui seem not to be used at all.

Yutang, Lin: THE WISDOM OF LAOTSE
New York, Random 1948.

The famous Chinese author made a pleasant interpretation, bordering on religious devotion. The book also contains a quantity of comments and explanations.

Printed in the USA
CPSIA information can be obtained
at www.ICGtesting.com
LVHW040342050823
754295LV00002B/368